SAVING OUR PLANET

CLEAN IT UP!

by
Mary Boone

PEBBLE
a capstone imprint

Pebble Explore is published by Pebble, an imprint of Capstone.
1710 Roe Crest Drive, North Mankato, Minnesota 56003
www.capstonepub.com

Library of Congress Cataloging-in-Publication Data is available on the Library of Congress website.
ISBN 978-1-9771-2581-1 (library binding)
ISBN 978-1-9771-2595-8 (paperback)
ISBN 978-1-9771-2601-6 (ebook pdf)

Summary: Introduces early readers to environmentalist concepts including greenhouse gases, carbon footprint, and air pollution, and what they can do to help the environment. Features real-life examples of kids who have made a difference.

Editorial Credits
Emily Raij, editor; Brann Garvey, designer; Svetlana Zhurkin, media researcher; Katy LaVigne, production specialist

Image Credits
iStockphoto: SDI Productions, 13, 20; Newscom: Zuma Press/Robin Loznak, 26; Shutterstock: Alexander Ermolaev, cover, Alexandros Michailidis, 23, Andrius Kaziliunas, 7, Anna Moskvina, 10, Dmytro Zinkevych, 29, Iakov Filimonov, 18, jaroslava V, 14, Magnetic Mcc, 15, Mike Jett, 25, NadyGinzburg, 5, PSD photography, 9, Rob Marmion, 4, Roman Mikhailiuk, 11, Tatiana Gladskikh, 19, wavebreakmedia, 16

All internet sites appearing in back matter were available and accurate when this book was sent to press.

Printed and bound in the USA.
PA117

TABLE OF CONTENTS

A Sick Planet 4

Why It Matters 8

Making Changes 12

Students Taking a Stand 22

Glossary 30

Read More 31

Internet Sites 31

Index 32

Words in **bold** are in the glossary.

A SICK PLANET

When you are sick, you try to get better. You rest. Maybe you have some soup. Your parents care for you. Earth is sick right now. People haven't been treating it well. But we can help it get better.

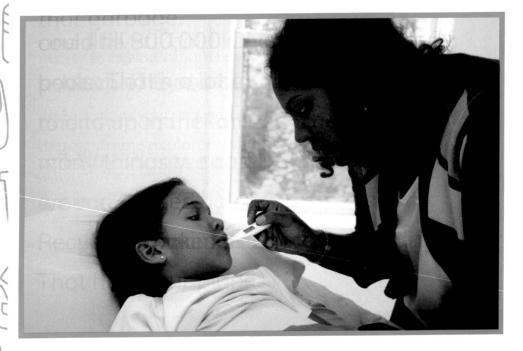

People have been throwing away too much trash. We have also been using too much **fuel**. Our actions are making the air, water, and land dirty. Cleaning up won't be easy. But lots of people doing a little can help.

We use a lot of energy every day. Factories need energy to run machines. Families use energy too. It takes energy to drive a car. Washing dishes and having the TV on take energy.

Some energy comes from burning coal, gas, and oil. That puts bad gases into the air. They are called **greenhouse gases**. These build up. When it rains, they go into the ground and water. They **pollute** the air. They trap heat around Earth. This causes **global warming**.

Polluted air in Los Angeles, CA

WHY IT MATTERS

One hot day is nothing to worry about. But Earth's temperature has been rising for a long time. This is called **climate change**. Our air is about 2 degrees Fahrenheit (3.6 degrees Celsius) hotter than 150 years ago. That little number is a big deal.

Warmer temperatures have a huge effect. **Glaciers** are melting. That raises sea levels. It causes floods. Storms are stronger. Summers are hotter. Droughts last longer. Wildfires happen more. Scientists think climate change is causing many of these events.

All people add to climate change. We throw out trash. We cut down trees. We use gas.

When you use energy, some bad gases go into the air. One is **carbon dioxide**. Your **carbon footprint** is how much carbon dioxide goes into the air because of you. The size of that footprint depends on your choices. You can make it smaller.

MAKING CHANGES

How can you help clean up Earth? Talking about climate change is a good start. Talk with your family. How can you use less energy? Turn off lights when you leave a room. Take shorter showers. Unplug electronics when you're not using them.

You need to go places. Can you walk to school instead of riding in a car? Carpooling helps too. Fewer running engines make less air pollution.

There are cleaner types of energy. They can come from the sun, wind, and water. This energy doesn't put out bad gases. And sun, wind, and water are all around us.

Solar panels turn sunlight into energy. Wind turbines make energy from wind.

Factories can switch to cleaner energy. So can you! Use LED light bulbs. These use less energy than other types. They also last longer. LED lights save energy and money.

Using less stuff cuts back on energy. Can you use less? Can you reuse more? Carry a reusable water bottle. Shop with reusable bags. Try not to buy things you only use once.

Think before you throw away. If you can't reuse something, can you give it to someone who can? If not, can you **recycle** it? Paper, plastic, aluminum, and many other materials can be recycled. They can get turned into clothes, furniture, and even jewelry.

There is a way to use new things to help the planet. Grow them! Gardening fights climate change. Plants remove carbon dioxide from the air. They also release oxygen we need to breathe.

Growing your food helps in another way. Big trucks carry food to stores. Many travel thousands of miles. Driving pollutes the air. Food from far away needs more packaging. That becomes trash. Less driving and packaging means a smaller carbon footprint.

Schools have carbon footprints too. Think of ways your school can reduce its footprint. What can you do in your classroom?

Talk to your friends and teachers. Can computers be turned off when not in use? Can you use less paper? Can you start a garden club? Maybe the club can grow food to give to families.

STUDENTS TAKING A STAND

Kids around the world are helping the planet. Greta Thunberg was a teenager in Sweden when she learned about climate change. She skipped school to stand outside government offices. She held a sign that said "School Strike for Climate."

Greta has become a climate **activist**. She talks to world leaders. She met with the Pope. She inspired four million people to join in a worldwide climate strike.

Greta Thunberg leads a march for protecting Earth's climate.

Isra Hirsi lives in Minnesota. She joined a school club to help the planet. Isra learned about climate change there. She wanted to spread the word.

Now she teaches others. She helps students get involved. Isra helped start the U.S. Youth Climate Strike. That group has planned more than 1,000 strikes across the country.

Isra Hirsi speaks at a strike in Washington, D.C.

Jamie Margolin wanted kids' voices to be heard. She knew leaders were talking about climate change. But she worried kids were left out. No one was asking what young people thought.

The Seattle, Washington, teen planned a youth climate change conference. Jamie wanted it to be so big it couldn't be ignored. In 2017, she started Zero Hour. The group teaches others to speak out against climate change. Zero Hour gives kids a voice.

Jamie Margolin (right), Greta Thunberg (left), and others sit in front of the U.S. Supreme Court building to call for change.

Earth takes care of us. We need to take care of it. Use less. Do more. Start at home. Spread the word in your neighborhood. Get your school involved.

Global warming and pollution won't go away overnight. But changes now will make a difference later. Help make those changes. Clean up the planet.

GLOSSARY

activist (AK-tuh-vist)—a person who works for social or political change

carbon dioxide (KAHR-buhn dy-AHK-syd)—a gas with no smell or color that people and animals breathe out

carbon footprint (KAHR-buhn FOOT-print)—the total greenhouse gases caused by one person or group

climate change (KLY-muht CHAYNJ)—a significant change in Earth's climate over a period of time

fuel (FYOOL)—anything that can be burned to give off energy

glacier (GLAY-shur)—a large, slow-moving sheet of ice

global warming (GLOH-buhl WARM-ing)—the slow rising of Earth's temperature

greenhouse gas (GREEN-houss GAS)—gas in a planet's atmosphere that traps heat from the sun

pollute (puh-LOOT)—to make dirty or unsafe

recycle (ree-SYE-kuhl)—to make used items into new products

READ MORE

Camerini, Valentina. *Greta's Story: The Schoolgirl Who Went on Strike to Save the Planet*. New York: Simon & Schuster, 2019.

Harkinson, Kim. *50 Things You Can Do to Save the World*. New York: Racehorse for Young Readers, 2020.

Roberts, Jack L. *A Kid's Guide to Climate Change and Global Warming*. Palm Springs, CA: Curious Kids Press, 2019.

INTERNET SITES

NASA Climate Kids: Big Questions
climatekids.nasa.gov/menu/big-questions/

National Geographic Kids: Climate Change
kids.nationalgeographic.com/explore/science/climate-change/

World Urban Campaign: Zerofootprint Youth Calculator
worldurbancampaign.org/zerofootprint-youth-calculator

INDEX

activists, 22, 24, 27

carbon dioxide, 10, 18
carbon footprints, 10, 19, 21
clean energy, 14, 15
climate change, 8, 10, 12, 18, 22, 24, 27

driving, 6, 12, 19

energy, 6, 10, 12, 14, 15, 17

factories, 6, 15
fuel, 5, 6

gardening, 18, 19, 21
glaciers, 8
global warming, 6, 28
greenhouse gases, 6

oxygen, 18

pollution, 6, 12, 19, 28

recycling, 17
reusing, 17

schools, 21, 22, 24, 28

trash, 5, 10, 17, 19

ways to save energy, 12, 15, 17
weather, 8